Money Lit
Activity Book

This activity book was inspired by the idea that kids begin flexing their money life skills learning muscles at a young age. The idea of financial literacy may sound boring, even to adults. I wanted to bring these concepts to kids in a fun way so they can learn as they play. This book is intended to education kids in elementary and middle school on the money life skills needed before they graduate high school. Money Lit offers other money life skills classes and materials to supplement this book. The activity book may also be used as a companion to a money life skills curriculum that parents can teach at home or on the go. If you are interested in more information on this curriculum or for more supplemental classes or materials: email us at: MoneyLitLearning@gmail.com or check us out on social media and send us a message there. Happy learning!

Thank you to the Plutus Foundation for the grant to make this activity book possible. The Plutus Foundation supports programs that enhance financial literacy, education, and empowerment.

Thank you to my illustrator, Kelly, for encouraging me along the way to create this book and for being a sounding board I could bounce ideas off of.

PLUTUS
FOUNDATION

Copyright © 2020 by Stephanie D. Pyke

FIRST EDITION

Human Capital

Definition: Skills, knowledge, and experience an individual has, and the value this can add to earning potential and their community.

My Skills are:

My Knowledge/Experience is:

If you had to make money just using the skills and knowledge that you have right now, what job would you do or what business would you start?

Would it be a good (item or product) you sell or a service you provide?

_____

_____

_____

_____

_____

_____

_____

_____

_____

_____

_____

_____

_____

ALL ABOUT MY HUMAN CAPITAL

We all have skills that are different from those around us. Not everyone is good at the same things. Fill in the spaces to see what makes up your knowledge, skills, and experience. What skills would you like to learn that you don't already have? Learn = earn.

I am learning to:

I like to do:

I know how to:

When I grow up I want to:

I want to learn:

I practice:

My favorite class is:

I want to know how to:

Welcome, I'm
"Name"

WHY IS HUMAN CAPITAL IMPORTANT?

Your human capital is a tool you use to earn money. The more you learn, the more value you will have to offer your future employer and community. You can also use this human capital to become an entrepreneur and start your own business . While you are young, your job is to gain as much education, skills, and experience as you can so you will be able to enter adulthood with the tools you will need to find a job or start your own company.

What do you want to do when you grow up?

Draw it here

Show Us Your Creativity

What colors would you use for this design? Color it in and ask your parents to email it to us at: MoneyLitLearning@gmail.com. Designs will be posted on our social media pages and the best design could win a prize!

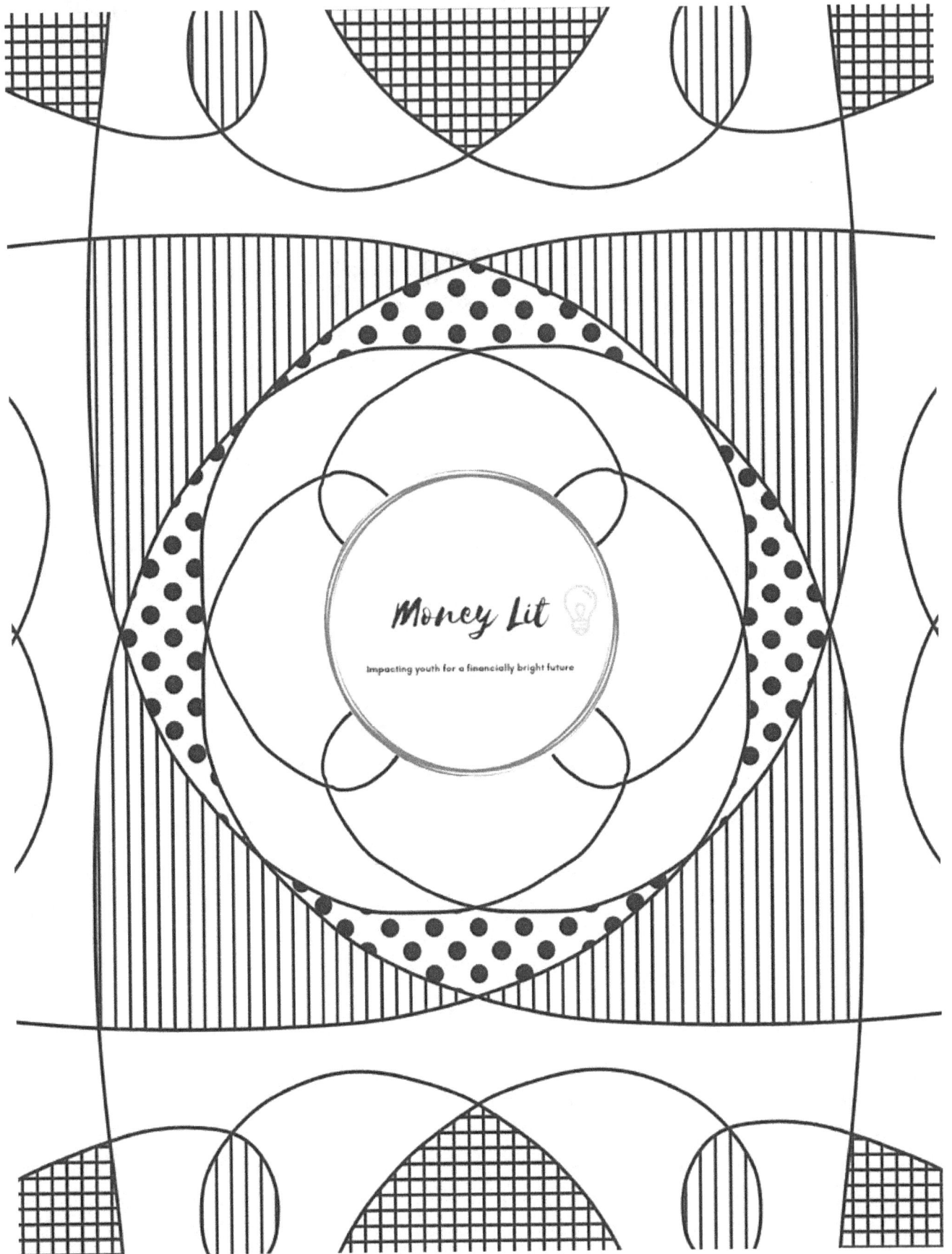

Money Lit

Impacting youth for a financially bright future

WHAT OTHER SKILLS DO I NEED?

We use our human capital skills to help our community in many ways. To get a job and help others we have to have more skills than just knowing how to read, write, or do math. We also have to know how to be on time, be kind, consider others, among many other personal skills.

I'M GOING TO USE MY SKILLS TO:

- ☐ Be a leader
- ☐ Help my community
- ☐ Be a good employee
- ☐ Start a business
- ☐ Invent something
- ☐ Other: _____

I'M INSPIRED BY:

(a teacher, a concept, a personal experience, a leader, etc..)

_____

_____

SKILLS I WILL USE TO BE THE BEST I CAN BE ARE:

cross out the ones you have, circle the ones you still need

being on time   kindness   saying "I'm sorry"   creativity   keeping a clean space

always learning   reading   flowing with change   communicating

considering others   teamwork   being truthful   problem solving

HERE IS A DRAWING OF SOMEONE THAT INSPIRES ME

Wants Versus Needs

Money is a limited resource. We have to work to earn our money, so we need to be careful with how we spend it. A good way to make wise spending choices is to decide what we have to have versus what we need to have. You always spend on your needs first.

Things I have to have	Things I want to have

ECONOMIC TERMS

Goods and Services

Goods: A physical item you purchase such as a car, toys, or food

Services: Actions someone provides for you such as mail delivery or hair cuts

In the space below, write "good" or "service" in the box in front of the picture

Taxi

Clothing

Bowling

Drinks

Hot Chocolate

Football

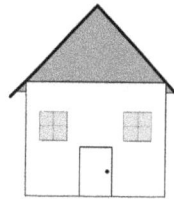

House

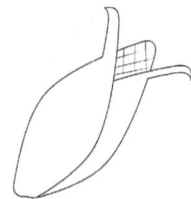

Farmer

Food Delivery

Movie Theater

DVD

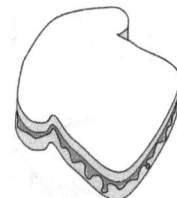

Restaurant

Shop Local

Browse the booths at your local farmer's market to find ingredients to make a meal for dinner.

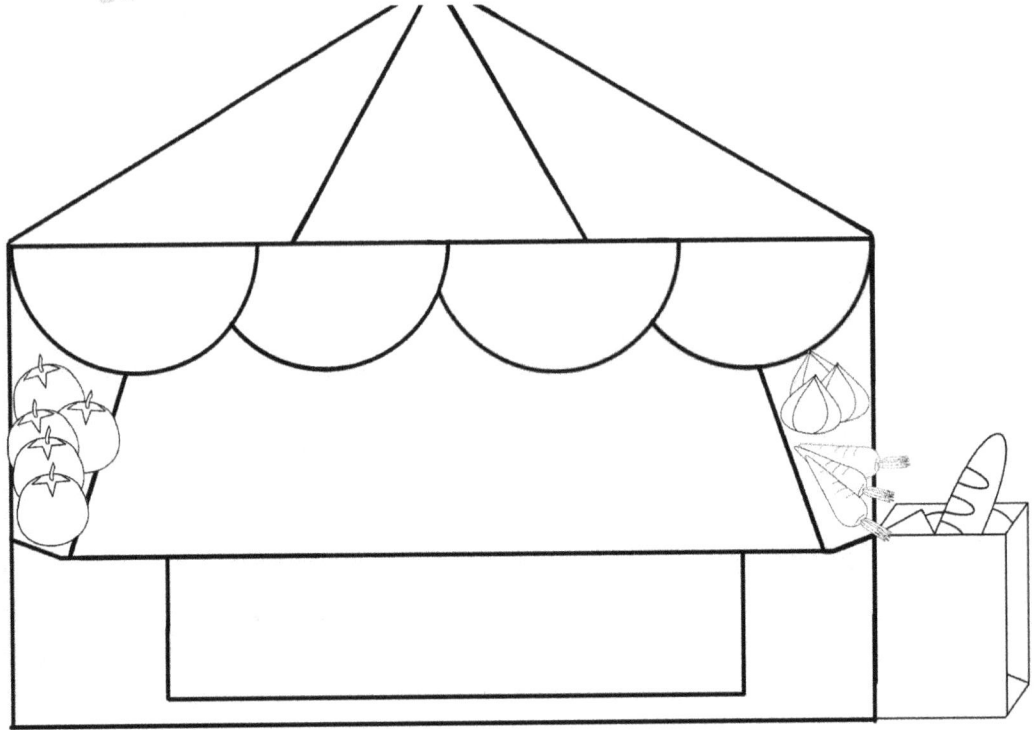

Farmer's Market

Shop Local!

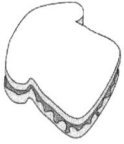

Let's Make a Meal

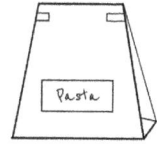

Using items found at the local farmer's market below, choose items to create a meal. Under "My Choices" draw in the food item you chose. Add up how much you spent in the space provided at the bottom on the page.

Main Meal

Grilled Cheese:
*Bread $5.00
*Cheese $4.50
*Butter $3.00
Vegan options
*Vegan cheese $6.00
*Herb Oil $5.00

Pasta:
*Spaghetti $6.00
*Sauce $5.00
Optional add-ins
*Meat $4.50
*Peppers $2.00
*Mushrooms $3.00

Side Options

Salad:
*Lettuce $3.00
*Tomatoes $2.00
*Cucumbers $1.00

Green Beans:
*Green Beans $3.00

Stewed Tomatoes:
*Tomatoes $2.00

Garlic Bread:
*Bread $5.00
*Garlic $1.00
*Butter $3.00
Vegan Option:
Herb Oil $5.00

My Choices

Write in the items you chose and add up how much it cost.

Item:	Cost per Item:	Total Cost:
	$	$
	$	
	$	
	$	

Build Your Own Booth

Use the market booth template below to "set up shop". What is something you would sell at your local farmer's market? Would you bake something? Create something? Sell something you grow? Let's see your creative earning idea. Put your business name on the sign and draw in your product or service you plan to sell. How much would you sell your product or service for?

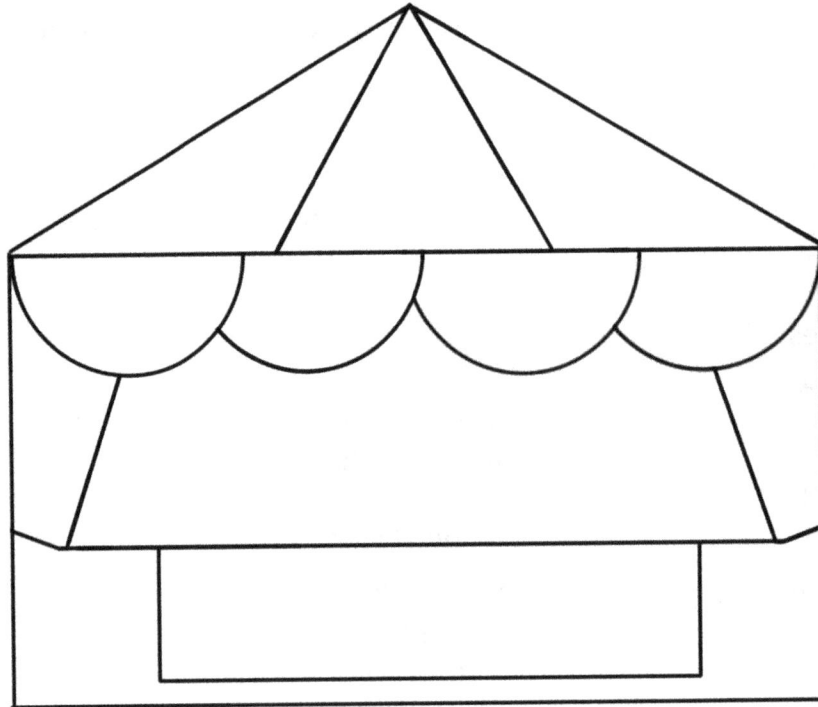

Simple Business Plan

Complete this worksheet to start setting goals for your big business idea!

My idea:

_____

_____

Marketing:

Customers (Who am I selling to?)

_____

_____

Promotion (How will I tell others what I'm selling?)

_____

_____

Finances:

Startup costs (What materials do I need to get started? How much do they cost?)

_____

_____

Profit = How much I charge - the cost of my materials (profit is the money you get to keep or invest back into your business)

_____

_____

_____

Design Your Logo

Design a logo for your product or service for your booth. This will help customers become familiar with what you are selling. In the business world, this is called branding. You want people to see your logo and know exactly who your company is and the product or service you offer.

Concept connection:
Think of your favorite mac n cheese. If someone showed you the box but covered up the words, would you still recognize the brand by the colors and box shape/size? What about your favorite fast food place. If you were driving down the road and saw their sign but their name was not on it, would you recognize which company it was anyways? How can you design a logo that represents your product/service so it is easily recognized in the same way?

Money, Money!

DO YOU HAVE A MONEY TREE?

Would you believe me if I told you I have a money tree in my yard? You are probably thinking "That is silly!" You are right. I do not have a magical money tree. While trees do provide us with many wonderful resources such as oxygen, shade, paper products, furniture, beautiful colors in the Fall, and so much more, trees that grow money we can pick do not exist. Money is a limited resource that we work to earn.

It is fun to be silly. Let's use our imaginations for a moment to pretend that a magical money tree does exist. Color in this money tree to show what your magical tree would look like if you had one.

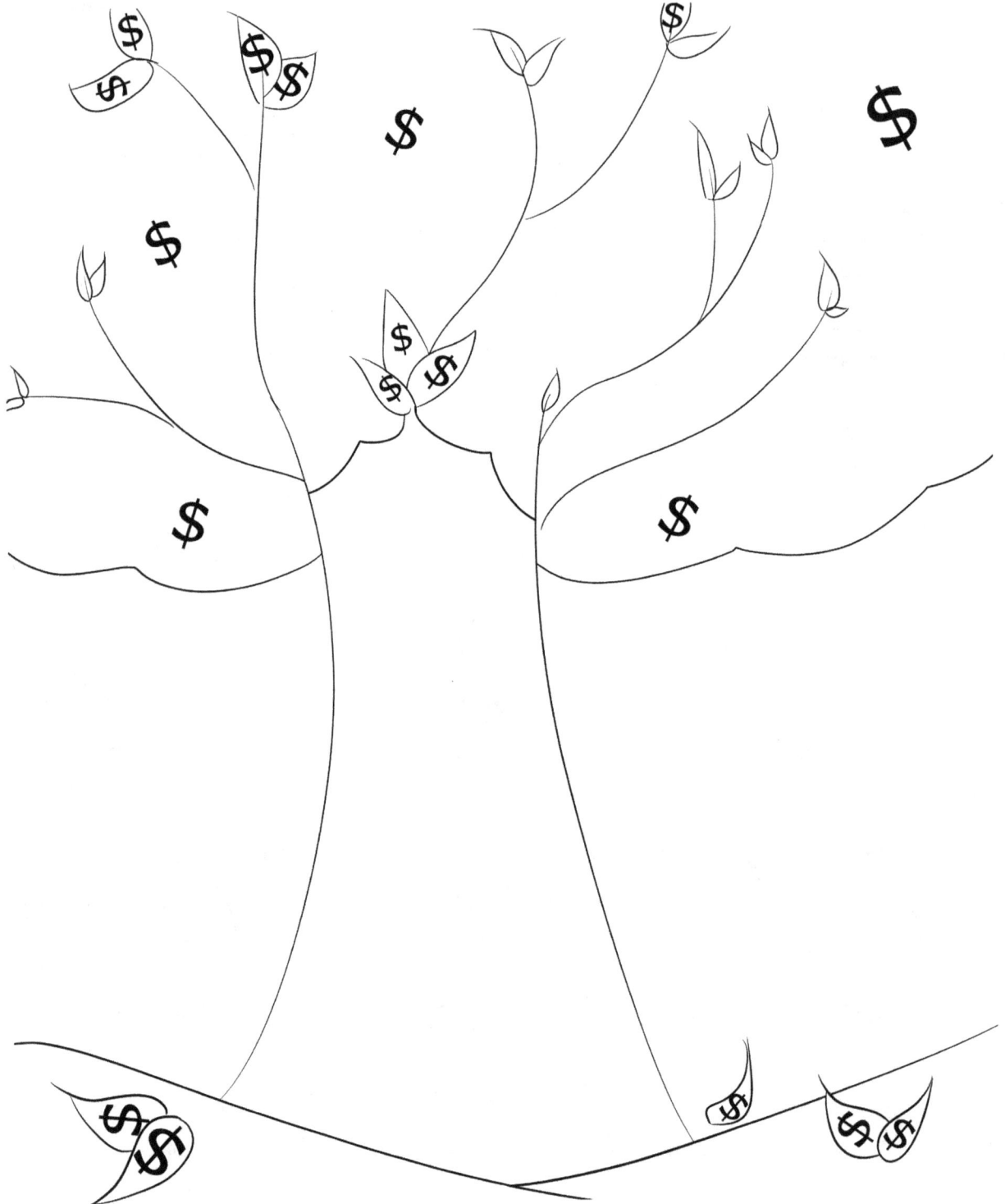

Color this historical train yard found in Chattanooga Choo Choo's Glen Miller Gardens

CHOICES AT THE SKATING RINK

Money is a limited resource so we must make choices when we spend our money.

You have $5 to spend at the skating rink on a snack and/or drink. Which snacks or drinks below would you choose? Circle your choice. How much did you spend?

I spent $_____

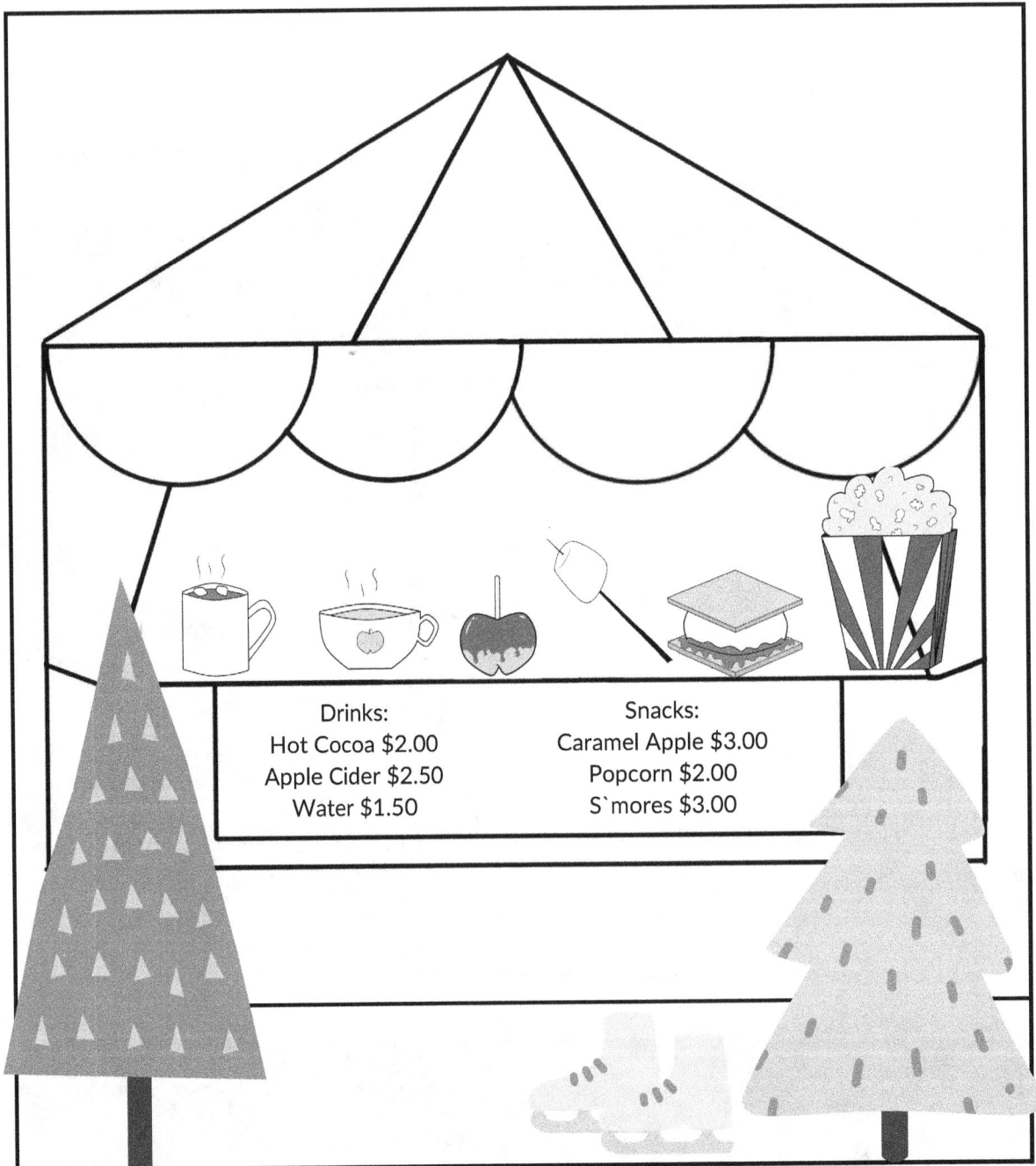

Drinks:
Hot Cocoa $2.00
Apple Cider $2.50
Water $1.50

Snacks:
Caramel Apple $3.00
Popcorn $2.00
S`mores $3.00

Opportunity Cost

Opportunity cost is the next best alternative that is <u>given up</u> when a choice is made.

Example: If I only have $5 and I want both ice cream, and lunch from a fast food place, I will have to choose one or the other. The one I don't choose is the one I gave up. The one I gave up is my opportunity cost, or the opportunity I didn't take.

Circle the best option to spend your money on between the two options given. Keep in mind what is the most you get for your money spend (money is a limited resource, once you spend it you don't have it!). What is your opportunity cost (the one you didn't choose)?

 $20   OR $30

 $15   OR $12

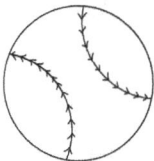 $15   OR $15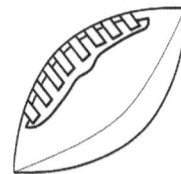

 $10   OR $10

 $1.50   OR $1

Cut Out Your Own Bookmark

Cut along the dotted lines and glue or tape the two pieces together to make a bookmark to use on your reading adventures. What reading adventure will you go on next?

Problem: State the problem

Alternatives: What are your options?

Criteria: What are the guidelines to consider?

Evaluate: Compare your alternatives based on the criteria

Decision: Time to make a decision

Have a choice to make?

Use the PACED method

Money Lit

Save Your Money

Money is a limited resource. We have to work to make it and once we spend it, we will have to work more to have more. We always have things we want to buy so we should save some of the money each time we earn so we have it when we need it.

Help this money find its way to the piggy bank to be saved for later wants and needs

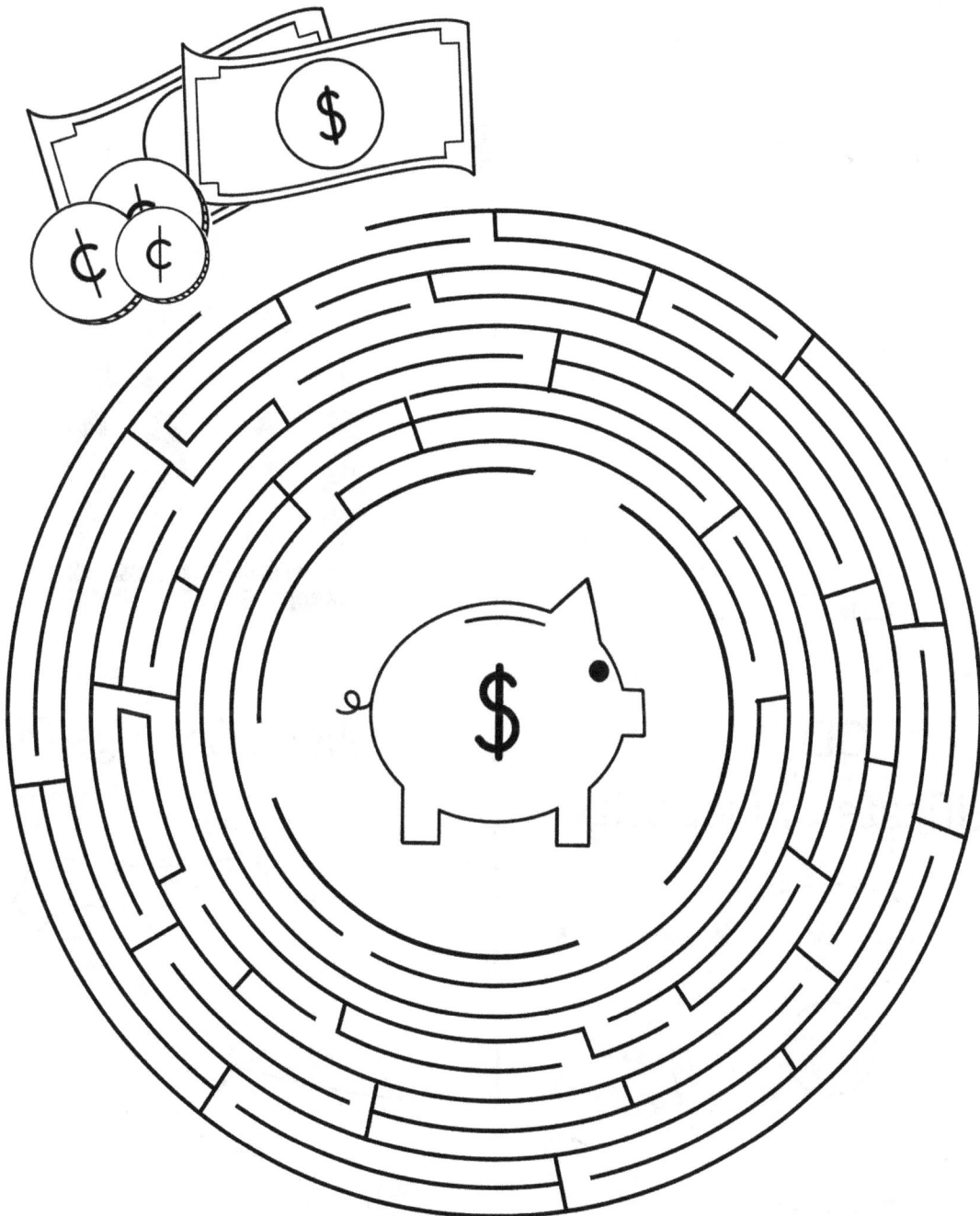

WAYS TO SAVE

*A piggy bank will hold your money. It won't make more money for you.

*A savings account at the bank will hold your money. You will earn a small amount of interest. Other people and companies will be able to deposit money into your account.

*A CD, or certificate of deposit, is a savings option at the bank that will earn more interest than a traditional savings account.

*A 529 college savings account is a place to save money for college. It has the potential to earn more interest than a traditional savings account at a bank. The money you save here can only be taken out when you are college age.

Piggy Bank

Savings Account

CD
(Certificate of Deposit)

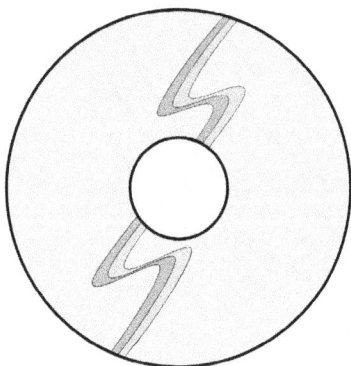

College Savings Plan

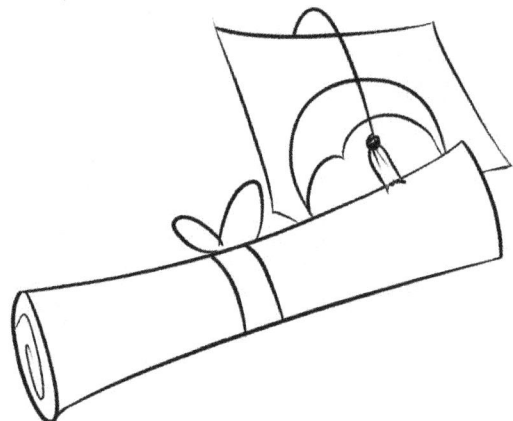

Savings Goals Bookmark

This bookmark is special. It will help you track your savings goals. What are you saving for? How will you earn the money to save?

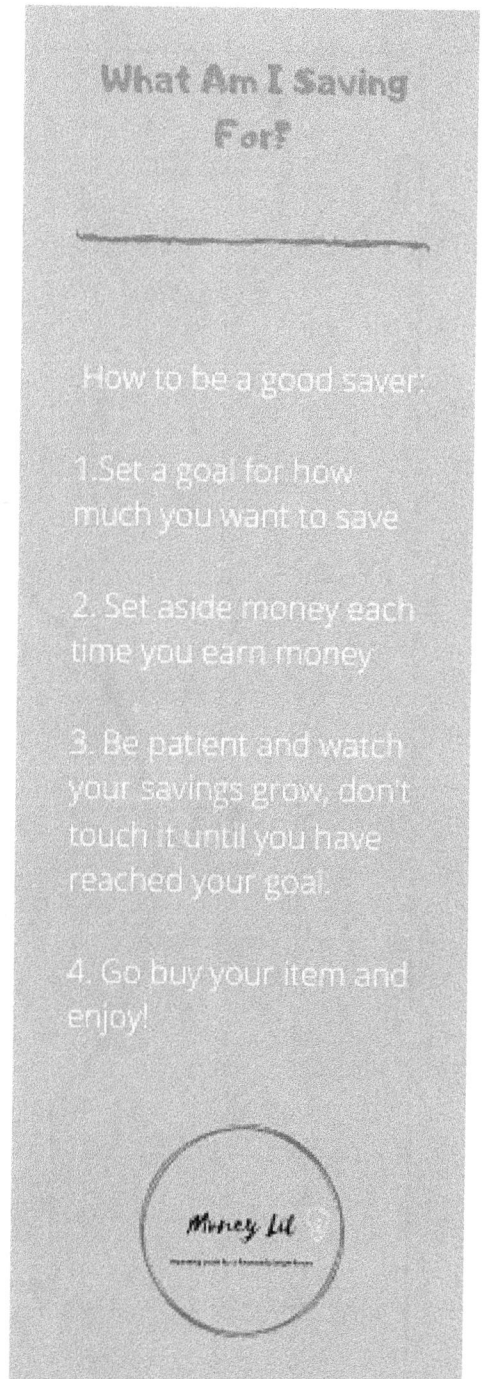

My Savings Goal

What Am I Saving For?

_____

How to be a good saver:

1. Set a goal for how much you want to save

2. Set aside money each time you earn money

3. Be patient and watch your savings grow, don't touch it until you have reached your goal.

4. Go buy your item and enjoy!

Money Lil

Design a Piggy Bank

Use your creative skills to design or
decorate a piggy bank in your own style

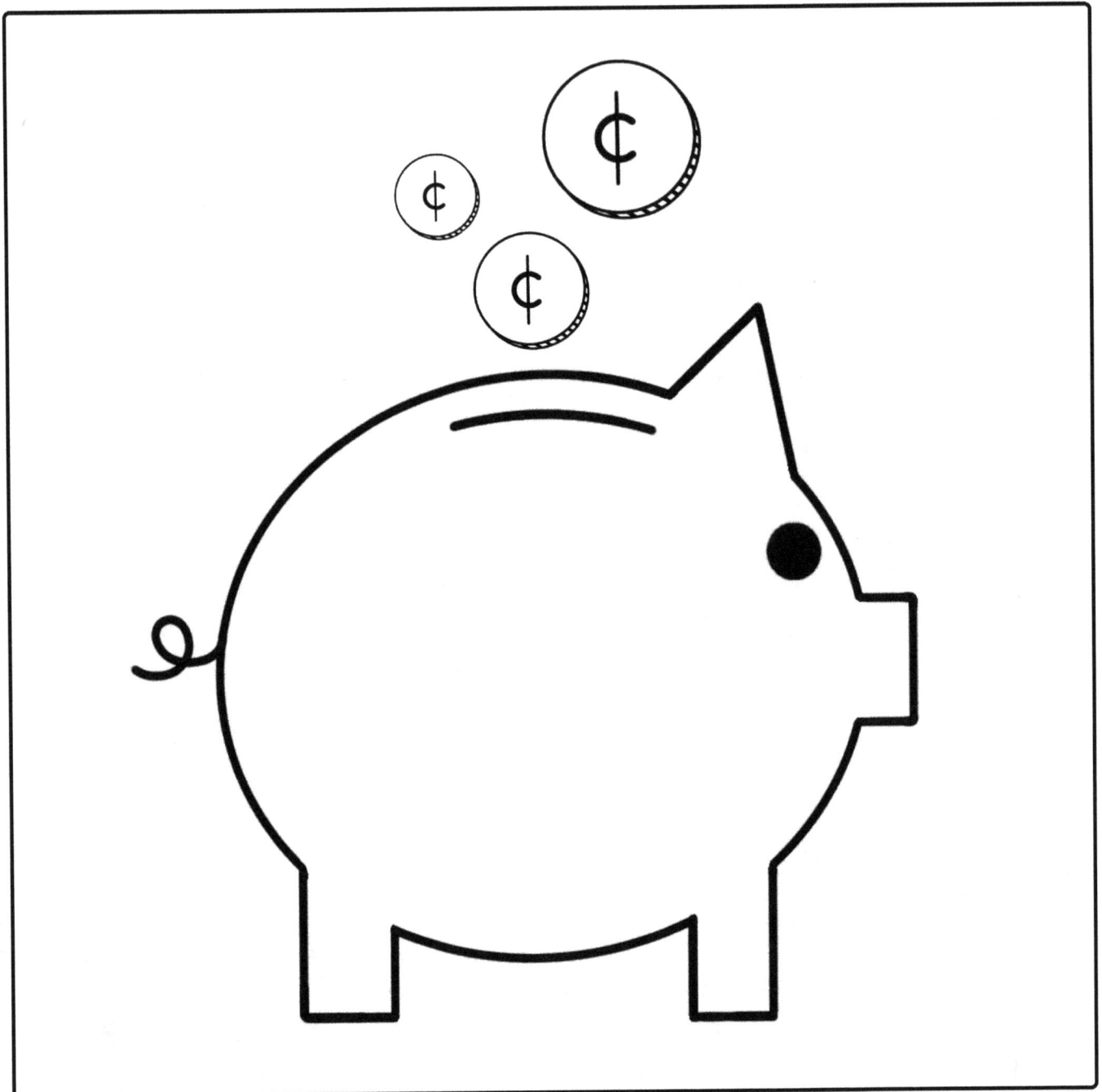

WHAT ARE DEBIT CARDS?

Have you watched your parents swipe a card when they pay for things? They could be using a debit card or a credit card. What is the difference?

Bank DEBIT

XXXX-555-5555

Exp Date   Your Name

Deposit Slip

Your Name
Address 1
Address 2
Phone Number

Date:
(Sign Here)

Bank Name
City, USA

ACCOUNT NUMBER

Cash >

$

A debit card is a card given to you by your bank when you open a checking account. When you swipe it to pay for things, you are spending money you have earned and deposited into your bank account.

Things you should know:
-Always check your balance before swiping your card. When you swipe your card and don't have enough to spend, the bank will charge you fees.

-You will need a special code to use your debit card called a pin number. It is four numbers that you may have to use when you swipe your card. You should never tell anyone other than your parents what this pin number is.

Do you have a checking or savings account?

_____

_____

_____

_____

When you earn money, how much of it do you save in your savings account?

_____

_____

_____

_____

WHEN TO USE A CREDIT CARD

A credit card is based on credit. Credit is a loan you take out against money you haven't earned yet. A credit card company allows you to do this based on trust. They look at how well you spend your money, and agree to let you borrow money when you swipe your card if they think they can trust you to pay it back.

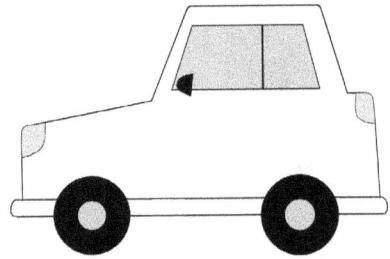

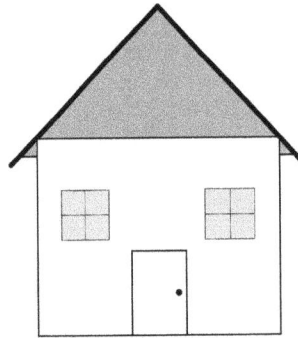

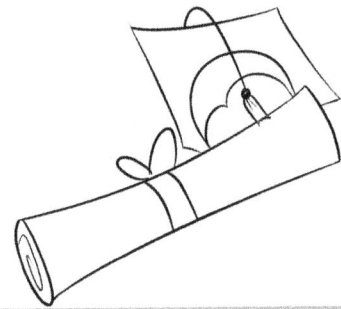

CREDIT

Bank

XXXX-555-5555

Exp Date   Your Name

What do we need credit for?

We use our credit when we apply for bigger loans to cover the cost of a car, a house, or paying for college. Sometimes we can plan and set a goal to save enough to pay for these things without borrowing money. Most of the time, these big expenses require us to take out a loan.

Things to remember when using credit cards:

-Credit cards charge interest, which is a fee based on a percentage of what you borrowed when you swiped your card. The interest compounds, meaning it grows daily and monthly.

-Always pay off your balance each month. If you can't do that, you shouldn't use a credit card. You will end up paying a lot more money for the item you purchased because of the interest you will pay.

-Always make your payment on time. This allows you to build trust which builds credit.

DRAW
YOUR GOALS

We build credit for things we want in the future. Draw the house or car you want to buy some day.

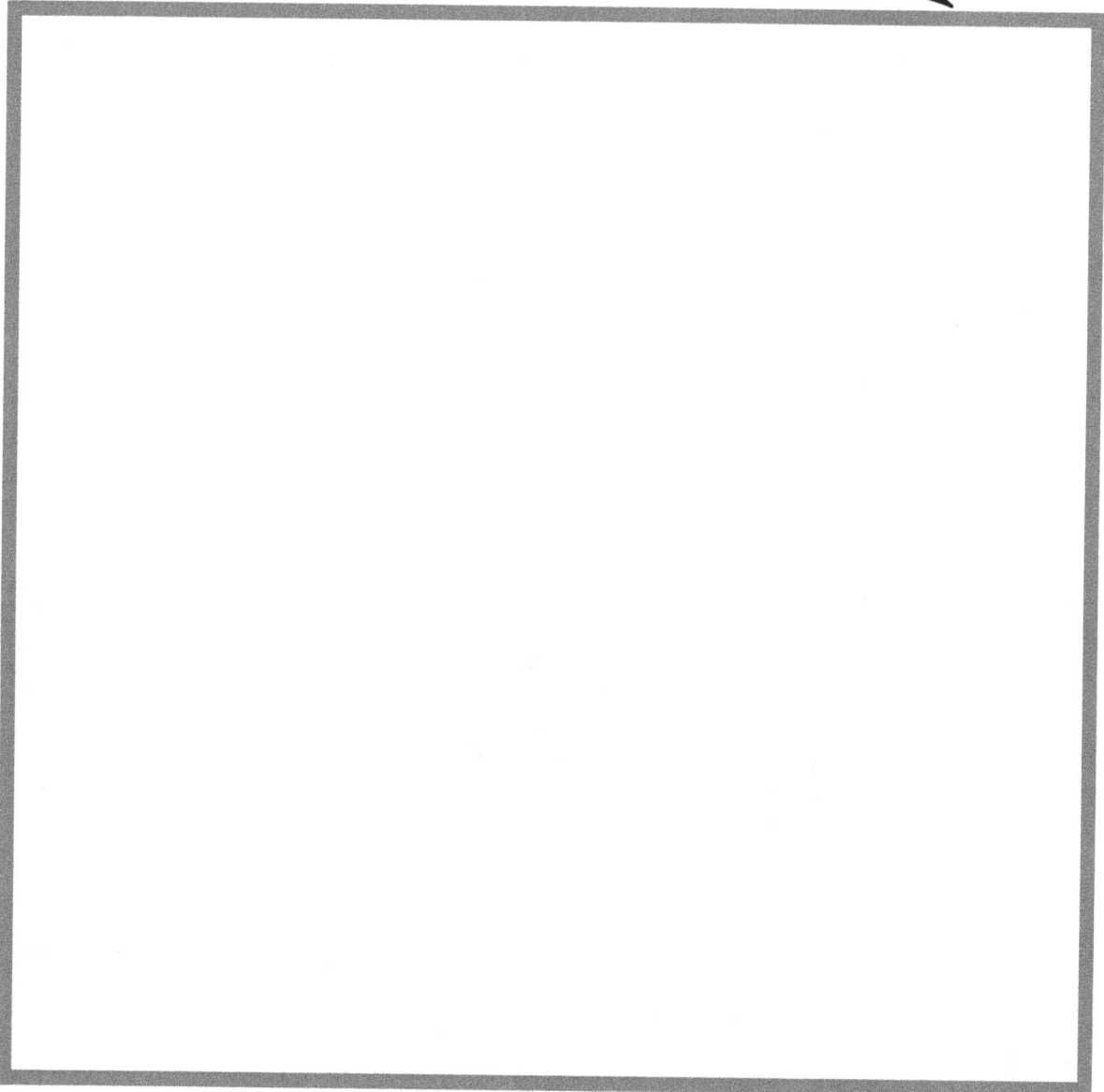

Cryptocurrency

Cryptocurrency is money that was created digitally to be spent or traded online. You can convert money from your bank into cryptocurrency and then you would put it into a digital wallet. A digital wallet is similar to an online bank but for digital coins.

The most well known cryptocurrency "coin" is Bitcoin. Some others you may have heard of is Ethereum, Bitcoin Cash, or Litecoin. People make money from cryptocurrency by trading its value against other cryptocurrencies or world currencies which can go up or down in value daily.

Color the digital coins below

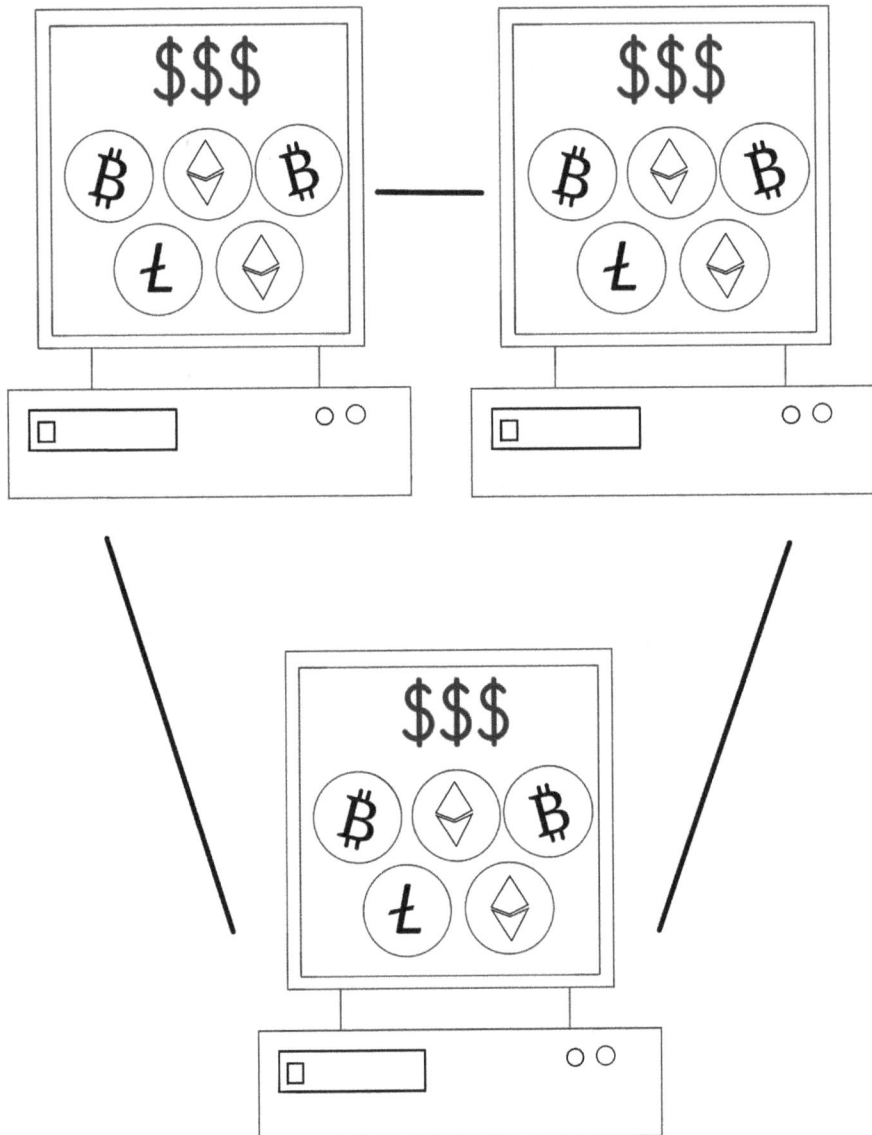

HOW DO I INVEST IN THE STOCK MARKET?

What is the stock market?
It is an online marketplace where people buy and sell stocks and bonds of larger companies. Companies make money by selling shares (a piece of) their company called stocks. When you buy or sell a stock, you are a shareholder of that company.

Instructions: Find several companies that you've heard about. Look up their stock history and pay attention to how often they are up or down. Write down several on this sheet to follow over the next month. Write down their value the day you choose to follow them, and then their value a month later. This will help you notice market trends

Company Name	Stock Value Today	Stock Value a Month Later

Pro tips: When considering stocks to invest in, you should research their company. Are they in the news in a positive or negative way? Are they opening a new location or putting out a new product? These things affect their values going up or down in the market. You should always be an active participant in your investing. It's your money so be educated, do your research, and stay involved.

When you are ready to invest, apps like Stockpile and Robinhood are great starting apps for kids! You can buy small shares of large companies in increments of $5 or $10. Once you have learned how the market works, you can take more risk.

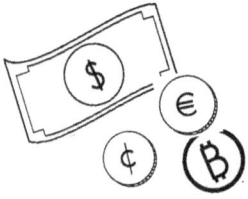

ECONOMIC CROSSWORD

Answer the questions and fill in the crossword with the correct answers. You will find answers to the questions throughout this workbook.

1   Money is a .... resource

2   What type of card is linked to a bank account?

3   The part of the business plan where you decide who your customer is

4   A .... tree doesn't exist, so we must save.

5   Skills, knowledge, and ability are .... capital

6   I should spend my money on .... before I spend it on wants

7   A business sells .... and services

8   Digital money